Musings in random order

Renuka Raghavan

BookLeaf
Publishing

Presentation by *BookLeaf Publishing*

Web: www.bookleafpub.com

E-mail: info@bookleafpub.com

ISBN:9789358312676

First edition 2023

The ordinary girl

She often sat with those legs long and tangled
In a tee that hugged her curvy love handles

She laughed aloud at every joke
Threw open her hair with a single stroke

Bindis would declare her very mood
But never did she wear it for an image 'good'

Her pallu fell off her shoulders quite carelessly
Just as her thoughts wandered rather aimlessly

She spoke her mind with no soothing balm
She stayed so calm and meant no harm

No regrets and zero guilt she had
That was why they called her bad

She got up late
And never once, was in haste

To tie her hair damp
Or then light the brass lamp

She prepared the dabbas and rolled the rotis
But promptly avoided being equated to 'devis'

She wondered why her 'follies' were
Often decided by those strangers there

Here and everywhere followed their eyes
Waiting to see her commit that vice

But they showered her neighbour with lots of
grace
Maybe because her dupatta was in place!

Slumbered existence

She hurriedly wore her purple sneakers
And plugged the pods into her ears

To catch pace with the chill in the air
That tingled through her messy hair

With hasty steps she scurried off the door
To quickly wave a 'ta-ta' to Kishore

Who'd be sitting beside the fogged window
In the rear seat of the bright yellow tempo

But as she saw the door latch settle
She heard her Samsung ringtone tinkle

"Oh i need to rush ... can you please make it
quick?"
"Only ensuring that the address is right!"

The courier service had called to check

Ah yes! It dawned upon her again!
That Kishore had left for college... and when!

It was the cricket bat that she had parcelled
To Chennai where he had last week settled

Such was life for her this week
Little moments of reminders meek

That popped her out of forgetful slumbers

Life was pausing and braking with a grin
That she wasn't really used to until then

Her son was her sole mantra and mission
Who provided her with the needed vision

To lead a life of hope, joy and strength
After many years of despair in length

When her daughter had been snatched away and
why!
Not pausing or waving her the final goodbye...

Just like the beach sand from under her feet
Had washed away with waters, so neat!

Easy recipes

Clearing the kitchen slab
She took the book again
'Cooking made simple'
From among the many stacked

Prep time 10 minutes
Cooking time 5 minutes
Serves 4
Pretty easy to follow, her face lit up

This recipe should do it
She said to herself
As it had careful measurements
Of turmeric, chilly and salt

But every time she cooked
Following the guidelines carefully
She kept feeling a miss
Of something quite potent

What was that one void
Even when the tips were diligently followed
Did we need more masala this time?
Or did I use a 'table' spoon instead?

Amma, I just don't know the reason why
My curries never taste faintly as yours
There was just then an eerie silence
On the very other end of the telephone line

Oh ! Well , that's really nothing my mollu
Next time try adding just an ounce of love
And don't worry if you add more than required
As it only tends to increase the flavour

Be patient with cooking my dear
Just like you need to do with love
It needs a bit of time and patience
But eventually will blossom and bloom no
doubt!

Moments

I rushed for the door
Not thinking twice
To wear my slippers
Or tie my hair

My baby was fading
In my arms
I knew not how
I knew not why

Crying since morn
And not staying calm
She was unwell
And clearly agitated

I measured those drops
Of antibiotics for her
She looked at me
And wailed out loud

"No mollu, amma is here"
I tried my best
And stroked her head
While kissing her cheek

But that was it
And she rolled her eyes
I saw them go
Right up and blank

A few moments ago
She lay awake
But all at once
She fell asleep

Then at the hospital
They set out the alarm
Where multiple doctors
Rushed to a room

My baby was revived
And had a beating heart
I thanked my stars
But was cautioned again

"She is under observation
For twenty-four hours
Until we can be assured
On how far she has come"

As though I was hit
By a shooting meteor
That lost its way
And flew astray

Just seventy-two hours
Was all it took
For my baby to go
Without even turning back

She was given no chance
To kiss me goodbye
How cruel was God
If he ever existed

I decided that day
That I'd be a stranger to him
As he never even once
Had thought of me
When he plucked my little girl
Off my lap...

Daal and rice

Half a cup of moong
A quarter of toor
An inch long green chilly
A pinch of haldi and salt

Our lives are but a bowl of hot daal
Poured over some parboiled rice
The left over from yesterday's feast
Bringing us to the status quo

That yesterday was gone
Tomorrow we know not
But today we have a choice
To make use of it best

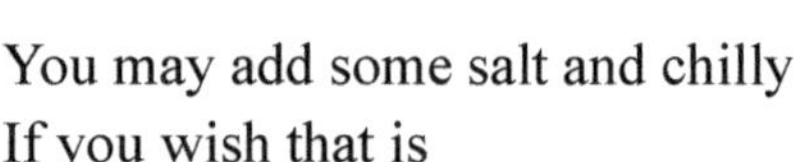

Life is but a bit of today
Soaked in a lot of yesterday
Quite like some left-over daal
Spicing up today's fresh rice

You may add some salt and chilly
If you wish that is

But don't forget
By any chance

To have it with
A dash of lemon!

Power puffs

The huge ashtray in the outdoors
Below the signboard that said,
'Smoking area'
The smoke they puffed off
Rose up in sync

Some were short
Others longer

Sharing life stories there
Brought comfort to their hearts

Ever since the 'no smoking' signs came up
They met there
They stood there
They smoked there
They had conversations there

Nicotine brought them relief
But temporary, they knew well

More than the early morning puffs
That they took upon arrival
That had a hurried, ' see you in the afternoon'

They looked forward to the lunch break one
That came at around 1 'O clock

Where they'd ask each other
'How was your evening yesterday?'

And exchanged mundane
Phases of their lives
Though starkly different
Was one from the other
They had many things
Quite in common

A longing to share a tale or two
With someone willing to listen
And not give them profound opinions
But simply hear each other through

Hot and spicy

The mushrooms turned smooth and shiny
As they simmered in the mozzarella sauce
I watched them soak as I added more cheese
Making them appear rather soft and soggy

My heart and mind had decided to sizzle
On my heavy-bottomed pan of heated emotions
They had been stacked away all this while
From the dust and smoke of everyday life

It would depend on the toppings I threw in
Whether to turn it savoury or sweet
I very carefully chose them hence
Not wanting to ever turn them bland

Life turned spicy, hot and sweet
All at once without the slightest hint

I wonder if the chillies and salt
All this while until now
Were sitting bored and aimless
In the meek corner shelf
Of the huge wooden cupboard

The sizzle will settle after a while I know
But I had already decided to stir them up
Whenever I'd need that zest in life
To pump things up and add more flavour!

Blanket pulls

The pull for the blanket
Is an everyday affair
That happens between us
Every night without fail

There are soft fluffy ones
Stored up in the closet
But we are stubborn to stick to one
As it is a sign of our very unity!

The beginning is calm
With equal and measured portions
A little more on one side
Really doesn't matter

But as the night progresses
We tend to gradually withdraw
Into our weirdest dreams
And start being ourselves

Beginning with a soft nudge
Or a very brief pull at first
Later it intensifies
Into a much stronger force

Thus we decide, the next day
That definitely without a doubt
We take an extra blanket out
As we simply need not fight
Over a large ball of wool

But as the night arrives
And we are in time for bed
Our emotions are soft and subtle
Not willing to divide ourselves now
Using two separate blankets, oh no!

Mortal thoughts

As I return home after work
I set my mind to the rewind button

Was it that mail that pulled the trigger?
Or was it the lady who countered my remark?

When I walked past the pantry room
Did I notice the men hiding a laugh?

The deadlines that were to be met
Appeared nearer than they actually were

An aching head was in the background
As I sat through the multiple meetings

Will I ever be content and satisfied
The day I decide to hang my boots?

Well.. it is but for time to tell
For we just wait for the big bright day

When things get better and lilies bloom
All at once at a single stretch
As if someone would strike them
With a big and bright wand!

Little big things

Waking me up with a hot cup of coffee
On that Sunday morning when I sleep like a
baby

Or maybe,
Allowing me to apply that final coat of lipstick
Even when you had dressed up ten minutes back

Or maybe,
Voluntarily correcting my sari pleats before we
left
Even though you were annoyed at how late we
already were

Little big things
Go unnoticed
By most of us
In our daily lives

But these are what matter
And make our lives better
When we feel the burden
That we carry on our shoulders

Not realising that time
Fleets off in a second

And leaves us all blank
Lost in regrets
Of why we never paused
And looked around

Soaking in the moment
And simply curling up
On the cozy blue sofa
Sipping that tall glass of wine.

A tickle that fleets

Like a wave at the beach
That touches your feet

Withdrawing after every touch
Love is today a fleeting emotion

An emotion that clearly begins
With a butterfly like sensation

Fluttering around you
Wanting to be noticed

Catching your sleeves
Later settling on your wrist

Entering your senses
Tickling you slowly

Leaving a scent soon enough
That is hard to wash off

Once it flies away
You run in search of it

Not knowing where to look
Not realising it is gone

So be wise and choose right
Build that armour and hold it tight

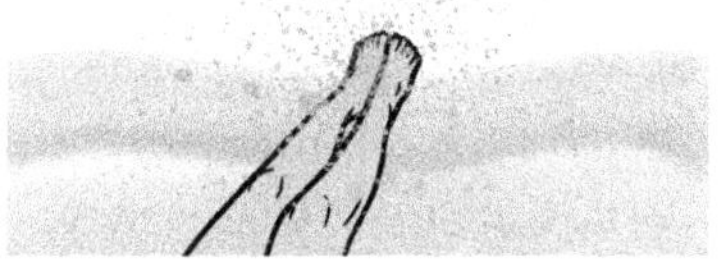

Dream on

How do you know you're capable
Asked little Sarah
Only when you try, honey
Said mama

So what if I try?
Asked little Sarah
Well if you try, you know your strengths
Said mama

And what if I know my strengths?
Asked little Sarah
When you know your strengths you work
towards your goals
Said mama

So what if I work towards my goals?
Asked little Sarah
If you work towards your goals, you reach your
dreams

Oh mama, do we really need to dream?
Asked little Sarah
Oh yes, honey, we all live to dream!
Said mama

Dreams are what takes us forward
Dreams are all that we have
No person in this world
Lives without a dream

For if there is someone like that,
He is dead in life
He lives an empty life
With no hopes to hold on to

Life is itself a dream, Sarah
Dream on, honey
'Coz dreams do come true
When we work towards them

And when they do come true
The others call it a miracle!

Tina's new calendar

As always she...
Was in a hurry
To catch hold of
The brand new calendar

The first thing she did
Ever since she remembered
At the start of every
Brand new year

When little, the little joys
Of whether she would wear
Her birthday dress to school
Of when school closed
For Christmas that year
And of when she'd get
To meet her cousins

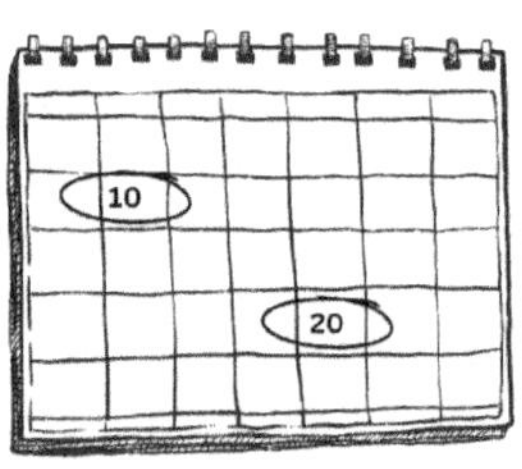

The new calendar
Was colorful
And sprinkled joy
With every turning leaf

As life progressed
The excitement settled

Anxiety took turns
With hope and faith

The red markers she made
For birthday reminders
Now filled up
With 'to-do' reminders

Life that was lived
Carelessly before
Well now it was
Planned and executed
To fit the cycle of bills
And timely payments
That growing up brought
Part and parcel of life

But still the thrill
Was always there
To mark
All the birthdays
Of those far and near
Friends and family

Bringing with it
Fleeting memories
Of the life that was once
Lived so fully

Hope , joy
And merry making
Was tightly squeezed-in
Even to this day
As her kids were watching
And she wanted them
To have eyes that filled
With hope and joy

As they would follow suit
And excitedly check up
Their brand new calendar..

The athaani or gate

The athaani
Was high for her
She had her share
Of luggage to carry

She saw how the sticks
Quite neatly placed
Much like rods
On their iron gate

But amma,
Is this as safe
As our iron gate
In the city?

Won't thieves come
At night when we sleep
With just one push
It could be broken down

And it wouldn't make
That creaky noise too!
Alerting us
When fast asleep

But amma laughed
Aloud at her question
And told her no one
Would do that here

We put up athaanis
For temporary stops
Maybe just
For the cow to know
That these are crops
And not munching grass
That grows all wild

If you look close
You see my dear
They are criss-crossed
Going this way
And that way

Not sturdy and strong
To keep people away
As we have friends
And no foes here

We slide two sticks
And easily pass
Just a bit of a pause
Before we go

It is but
Just a reminder
That Gopalan stays here
And Abdu stays there

The music app

As I installed the music app
I wondered what I'd play
Had thousands of songs at my fingertips
By the click of a button

They played one after the other
As though waiting for their turn

Playing music has evolved
And how!

After a long tired day
As I sit in my balcony
With the coffee mug in my hands
I play the music in the background

And that sets the whole mood

Do I play a slow keerthana first
Or maybe a quick Shakira!
Should I set the mood for melancholy
Or do I play the Rasputin

The day's events unfold
In a quiet and controlled rhythm

Just as the words flow out
Through the black Harman speaker
That sits behind the lamp
Bringing relief to my tired brain
That has slogged all day..

Music is a balm, a blessing
Music is therapy!

Blurred squares

His steps were slow ,careful and measured
He seemed as though he held them treasured

He moved about not blinking a twinkle
His forehead gathered a pensive wrinkle

His toothbrush amused him forever
His ink pens never met him for once

He saw his bedroom towards the right
He saw his bathroom just in sight

He left the front door open that day
But missed the shoes and sandals on the way

He forgot his shirt with labelled pockets
He instead wore his home-wear tees

When someone called out a familiar name
He looked around to see who came

He failed to see the sun turn moon
And lost count of the passing hour

His greetings met a cheerful stranger
But never once did he feel any danger

Then someone came up to him, near
Mashe, what is it that brought you here?

He knew not why people looked him straight
He felt as if he was trapped by some bait

He wished them well and walked beyond
He failed to process the confusion around

His family worried and hadn't known
When he had left, sometime at noon?

"For his mindless walk, they complained aloud"

But it was bound to be his last
Aimless walk beyond the gate

His rules were set and decided that day
His doors were bolted and keys were hid

His thoughts kept going in circular motions
His words had lost all their connections

He stared at the wall totally feeling blind
That was what he felt inside

It all began when he failed to name
His very own wife, his only companion

It struck his puzzled colleagues at work
When he missed a few zeros on those cheques

He sensed a chill and went totally still
A sense of calm but of unnerving sorts

Life had felt blurred
Since that very day
Nothing seemed right
In any shape!

The green saree

I go shopping these days
Searching for comfort
As in what I wore
I felt a queen

And queen I say
As in elegance and style
No, not in opulence
Or studded stones!

There was a time
When I wanted to grow up
Just to wear sarees
Like my amma wore

My amma's sarees
Were memories woven
Around seven yards of cloth
Starched and pressed

She was particularly so
Straight and organized
Had them neatly stacked
Away in the cupboard

As time went by
I grew particularly fond
Of a certain saree
That was a parrot green

It had a few tassels
On the sides
And embroidered prints
Here and there

The saree itself
Exuded class
That came from the times
She wore them in style

It was probably her character
That I fondly admired
And rightly so
Effortlessly imbibed

The little me
Was still in me
And so I insisted
On borrowing it from her

Amma your sarees
Are simply treasures
From the beautiful days
That you gladly lived

Ammayi's filter kaapi

The steel coffee filter
Sits quiet on the granite slab
Where it promptly gets to work
In the deep hours of the night

Catching the coffee essence
Drop by drop
Creating pure magic
As we all are, well asleep

The froth that brims
At the silver glass tumbler
Reminds me of my aunt
My very own Madras ammayi

Her coffees were made
Out of carefully roasted beans
Delivered to her
From the gardens of Munnar

She bought them annually
When visiting her relatives
She was particular about the aroma
Never compromising on its quality

Certain things dawn upon me
While I sip my instant coffee
That doesn't do justice
To my ammayi's filter kaapi

But I should definitely agree
That my store bought instant coffee
Has the amazing properties
To transport me in an instant!

To my ammayi's house
Right there in Madras

It provides me with comfort
And tons of memories
That come rushing to my mind
As I sit staring at my mails

Taking a break once in a while
I blow the piping hot coffee
And think of my ammayi
And her peculiar ways

The balcony chair
The warm sunlight that seeps in
The Gayatri mantram in the background
These were non negotiables
When sipping hot kaapi

At Ammayi's home in Madras

How food can transport
People in an instant
Especially tastes like these
That were with you when little..

Futile plans

Be brave they said
Be strong they whispered
Time is the biggest healer
This too shall pass...

My thoughts were frozen
As I looked outside the window
The cars were fleeting
The lights were flashing

Nothing seemed to pause
No one seemed to notice
How lonely I felt
After all the struggle

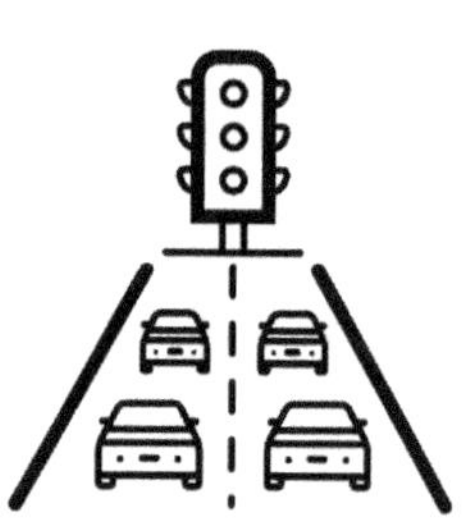

Life returned to normal
For everyone around
But I was caught in between
Feeling totally numb

Not able to feel a thing

My eyes were dead
My ears were deaf
My legs were stiff

My heart was broken

I looked around
And sensed no relief
In what I saw
And what transpired

Life would move on
With no change of plan
Everything was decided
We only had to live

Building dreams again
And working towards it
Not knowing a thing
About the future ahead

We have no say
We have no voice
In this vicious cycle of life
Where our days are weighed
And actions measured

As though someone somewhere
Was testing and timing
Our days beyond
To his own liking..

Silent battles

Sitting on my easy chair
That evening quite lazily

The warm setting sun
Had me sweating lightly
As the old ceiling fan
Had given up its might

The lone house lizard
Had lost its mind
As it sneaked up its way
Into the warm light's folder

Life had taken a back seat
As I shifted gears to neutral
Unfastening the seat belt
Very religiously worn

I started the engine again
Willing to give it a chance
Hitting the accelerator
My car sped straight

Just then the stop lights surfaced
Rather ridiculously on a highway!
Forcing me to brake the car
That went on high-speed

The sudden gear shift
Left things out of control
Leaving my sturdy vehicle
Shocked and confused

The crash was harsh
Leaving my bones broken
I picked myself up
But life had lost control

Beaten badly this time
It was hard to start afresh
Seemed a lost battle I was fighting
With battered hopes and a dejected soul

I picked myself up, yet again
Preparing to walk with a heavy heart
But my body was weak and spirit beaten
And at last I sat down to rest

As I had lost the battle

The whistling cooker

He built up strength
Under enormous vacuum

Whistling through
His only gap
Struggling to hold
His belted cap

Stuffed with vegetables
And some water
He pumped his breath
Slow and steady

The carrots and potatoes,
Shrunk and softened
When he remained
Mighty strong

Building in depths
An explosive pressure
That had to be released
Right in time

He blew out whistles
Keeping a count

He was deep and warm
Right from within

His mounting pressure
Had to be tamed
The fire was put off
And he was left to cool

Things were under control
He had settled by then
His cap was removed
And pressure released

Working well
Through and through
You find him at work
In every kitchen

The main man at work
At any Indian home.